Advance Praise for *We Are Not Where We Are*

"Who among us has not felt the desire to live deliberately? To disappear for a time, literally or figuratively, into the woods? Or, better yet, to somehow learn to breathe underwater. Working from Thoreau's own words—for the words don't lie—Matt Donovan and Jenny George have excavated and complexly reimagined what it might mean to awaken the self, if only fleetingly, to the self, to dream ourselves more fully into memory and history, to open ourselves more intimately to the world around us, and to perhaps almost touch what might lie below and beyond. *We Are Not Where We Are* is an encounter with between-ness. At once fresh and timeless, this collection is a mesmerizing exploration of the unsolvable mystery of being alive."

—Kathleen Graber, author of *The River Twice*

"Reading *We Are Not Where We Are* is an uncanny experience. It's as if, via the operations of erasure, Donovan and George have conjured the ghost not of Thoreau but of the Walden text itself. And what does this ghost have to tell us, and Thoreau too, if his spirit can hear it? That Walden is not a setting but 'a thought welling up,' Thoreau's 'I am   cock-crowing / to fill the pauses.' 'I should not talk so much about the title and critique of the book's most exhilarating erasure, one that enumerates the ways in which, still, despite any I's intervention, 'The earth is all alive and   sensitive... peopling the woods with larger life / and frog   and song   and bloom   and blow   and the coming in.'"

—Dana Levin, author of *Now Do You Know Where You Are*

"In poem after poem of *We Are Not Where We Are*, an erasure of Thoreau's Walden, Matt Donovan and Jenny George enact what erasure, as a conceit, is so capable of producing—dialogue, collaboration, criticism, and challenge. The title suggests an emphasis on locating, and these poems effectively unearth a speaker in search of an actualized self and an understanding of that self in relation to the natural world and fellow humans, all while utilizing Thoreau's contradictory and often problematic logic and imagination. In a way, their chapbook achieves precisely what Thoreau was perhaps after in Walden—it preserves something of beauty, form, and permanence in the world. Yet it also embraces flux, grief, and flow."

—Nathan McClain, author of *Previously Owned*

We Are Not Where We Are

We Are Not Where We Are

An Erasing of Thoreau's *Walden*

Matt Donovan

&

Jenny George

BULL CITY PRESS

Durham, NC

We Are Not Where We Are

Library of Congress Cataloging-in-Publication Data

Names: Donovan, Matt, author. | George, Jenny, author. | Thoreau, Henry David, 1817-1862. Walden.
Title: We are not where we are : an erasing of Thoreau's Walden / Matt Donovan & Jenny George.
Identifiers: LCCN 2024037580 (print) | LCCN 2024037581 (ebook) | ISBN 9781949344592 (paperback) | ISBN 9781949344608 (ebook)
Subjects: LCGFT: Poetry.
Classification: LCC PS3604.O5673 W4 2025 (print) | LCC PS3604.O5673 (ebook) | DDC 811/.6--dc23/eng/20240819
LC record available at https://lccn.loc.gov/2024037580
LC ebook record available at https://lccn.loc.gov/2024037581

Published in the United States of America

Cover art: Kent Rockwell, Dublin Pond, 1903, oil on canvas, 28 x 30 in., Purchased with the Winthrop Hillyer Fund, Smith College Museum of Art, Northampton, Massachusetts, SC 1904.2.1

Book design: Spock and Associates

Published by
BULL CITY PRESS
1217 Odyssey Drive
Durham, NC 27713

www.BullCityPress.com

Contents

We Are
Not Where
We Are

Every child begins the world again, to some extent

My arithmetic was   seeds
a few wild apples

Such   an interval   between me and
the recollection I had of it

winds passed over
the outside of the earth every where
I myself   suddenly   neighbor to those
mist   by degrees   revealed

I looked between   the blue   portion
place and time were   nearer
I was really there

I got up early and bathed in the pond
from within   its fruit

who does not believe that each day contains
an earlier

There is a dawn   in me

In most books the I, or first person, is omitted

the   I
drunk   through the summer
with   beans to hoe

the   I
on tiptoe
forever repeating
our   words

how it did run
and stumble and get up
and go on!

for all the world
with saucer eyes
my   I

I confess
sucking the pap of
the   I

It is true, I never assisted the sun materially in his rising

But   I often did better

I sat   and   grew

ticking   forward   the passing day

A man   without   end

setting   the grass

making   the pines and hickories

pushing up through the embankment

pushing out   from dry sticks

which had seemed to be dead

stirring   the glassy surface of the pond

my   out-of-the-way   I am

unfolding   amid the mountains

the   I am   blowing   through

woods   without   stopping

whirled along like leaves   run wild

Now   more alone than ever

my   I am   cock-crowing

to fill the pauses

clear and shrill for miles

reaching up to your   sills

under your windows   breaking through

into your cellar   rubbing

against the shingles for want of room

Such is the universal law

Bullfrogs   half a mile distant, or
just at my door

vast circuit

I have my horizon   I have, as it were
a whole earth
Every little pine needle

What sort of space is it
two minds   ?

I went through the darkness   whose work we are

the ocean of intelligences
I   the driftwood,   the sky looking down
a certain   doubleness

I love to be alone

We are never alone

I would fain say something

—we could not speak low enough
to be heard   as when   two stones
into calm water   break

we are merely   breath
all animal
commonly   bodily

we cannot
we cannot say

but there was room enough
within   the great solitude
into which the rivers   empty

chickadees
in the pine   the sound of praise
in disguise

The life that had laid torpid began to stretch itself

It waked and at length began
pacing slowly backward and forward
over the millet grass

reins loosely hanging in festoons

It sometimes was rattled by
the wilder fields
the pond holes in the woods
and pastures and swamps
though not in a bad sense

Near at hand,
upon the topmost spray of a birch,
it leached ashes

It remembered
with as much pity as pride
falling from time to time
at the other end of the town

I have sometimes had a vague sense of It
as a vast bellows

I might add
It matters little comparatively

Cast-off griefs are an atmosphere

in the woods
among the pines
I hardly ever failed

I   was   like Orpheus
who   was never cast away
nor distressed in any weather
and   was   guided rather
by his feet than his eyes.

not till we have lost the world
do we begin
to find ourselves

the grass
when the wind passes
bends

It is best to avoid the beginnings of evil

We were in total   unknown
surrounded by thousands of
nocturnal fishes   dwelling   below uncertain
queer   vast   spheres

With divided vision, I discerned
a single "body"
limbs   magnified and distorted

I   looked   through the hole,
I saw   the pulse of   the white   transparency
Some think it is bottomless
clean and bright like   stones

nations have   passed away
driven out of   the first water
their footsteps   rising and falling
just after a light snow had fallen,
appearing   unobscured

The snow reprints,   in clear   white type
some trace of this

Once there was no   here, and now there is
and this fable does not conflict
with the account   of the stones

a thousand years ago
the earth's eye   reflected
the whole silvery arc
the equilibrium of the whole

a water bug making   two diverging lines   that
the mirror   continually repairs

Now, here is Walden
a thought welling up

It is, after all, always the first person that is speaking

I set out one afternoon   a poet
when I found myself suddenly
uninhabited:—
        a Field
a Field!
before some fresh impulse
had altered it

Some have asked what I got to eat

I wished sometimes
Whatever I might speak of
carried a mistake
The true harvest of life

Yet, for my part, I was
only wise

Ah, how low I fall
compelled to eat and drink
the truth

The soul has a taste for
the fruits of disgrace

How happy's he who can say
impurity will descend
into his body and redeem it

If I had remembered this it would have prevented some mistakes

Sometimes   the   wonder   is   lost

I think that I am near the end of it

Angle-worms   ground-nuts
johnswort   grass
I was   a-fishing   into the essence of things
What was   I   thinking   ?

I held still   in a pine   In June
and heard the whir
of   The   mind

afterward   I   ate my lunch

You   sit   fastened
to   shame
the   day   threaded   brownish-gray
and   There is no   wild   if   rippling

the woods   sometimes
muzzle   prayer

To increase the warmth of our bodies by addition

Being hard, dark, and transparent   the night
flying low over the woods
surrounded me

I endeavored to keep a bright fire within

I grieved with   a grief   that warmed me   twice—
once while I was
level with the earth   with the dry leaves,
and once   while I was a   clear flame

I thought that I would just look in the window
and see   if the house was on fire

My whole body began to   go   forgotten,
a concealed   companion
You can always   see a face   in fire
in the unequal light

The mass of men lead lives of quiet desperation

I   spent some   winter evenings
while the snow whirled
making a path through
the former occupants of these woods

inhabitants

Cato Ingraham

who gave

Zilpha

the Walden Woods   a voice   that

Brister Freeman   and Fenda, his wife,

the Statten family

history   set on fire

fire that   leaped the brook

And   fresh sparks went up

and we   heard the crackling

and   felt the heat

and   concluded to let it burn

Wyman the potter

Hugh Quoil

Fix not thy heart of that which is transitory

except   a   moose-yard well trodden,
overhung by oak woods

pines bent down with snow

the   syllables   of winter
and   cat-owl
and   horizon

and   in the moonlight
One   time
the whole   wild   shore
of   short-lived
Near at hand
you

In short, I went on thus for a long time

After a still winter I awoke
—where? Daylight
Snow lying on the earth

Then to my work in search of
the liquid and trembling surface

Making a little hole
with breath   the pines
the stones
the sky
all animalized   beneath the rattling

It is remarkable the sound
of the bottomless

I should not talk so much about myself

The earth is all alive and   sensitive
The ice in the pond begins to be honeycombed
rains are melting the   exhausted winter   gradually
swelling and increasing   like a vast body   coming in to settle
the whole sound   made by its melt
and the sun dispersing the mist   and rivulets   and clay
and sometimes bursting through and overflowing   little streams
and leaves   and lichens   the original forms
and the whole   springing into existence
and energy strewing   and the animal body   and rivers
and insects   and branch and branch again
forward from the thawing mass   a little silvery system   and a drop
of the flow   a drop of   the drop   and a new leaf
coming out of the ground   and Earth-clothes
and heaps   and   flowers and fruit   metals   and music
and goldenrods, pinweeds, and graceful wild   meadow-sweet
and the earliest birds   and wool-grass   and relation   and the   !
and   !   and the grass   on the hillsides   all watered
and mild   and instantaneous   and the clouds   and the dripping

and the transparent pond   calm and full of reflecting
and brighter, greener, and restored   and mutual
the rush of wings   geese through the mist
peopling the woods with larger life
and frog   and song   and bloom   and blow   and the coming in

Conclusion

here is not all the world

Direct your eye right inward and you'll find
only   Walden ice
and   stick after stick

we are not where we are

The life in us is like   land
where we   began to   realize all this

Authors' Note

"I lived alone, in the woods, a mile from any neighbor, in a house which I had built myself, on the shore of Walden Pond," Thoreau writes in the opening of *Walden*, a book that is undeniably central to the American literary canon, as well as deeply flawed in its beliefs about individualism, the natural world, and forms of relation between people. If Thoreau's engagement with nature and experiment in solitude might afford opportunities for self-reflection about our current ecological disasters and technological addictions, for example, it's also well-worth interrogating his relentlessly patriarchal language, assumptions around land and belonging, and habitual surges of racism. As an act of collaborative intervention, *We Are Not Where We Are* was inspired both by the ways in which *Walden* continues to ensnare the American imagination as well as its inherently problematic nature as a text.

Our rules for creating these erasures were simple. The central chapters of *Walden* were divided equally between us and follow the order of the original text. All removed words and passages are indicated by a uniform length of blank space, and we didn't change any of Thoreau's original language or the order of his words on the page. Rather than create a blackout poem from the book's long introductory chapter, "Economy," we instead appropriated passages from that section for the titles of our pieces. "Conclusion," the book's final chapter, was created together as a collaborative blackout poem at Jenny's kitchen table.

Acknowledgments

Many thanks to the editors at *Blackbird* and *The Massachusetts Review* where some of these poems previously appeared.

Blackbird

"Every child begins the world again, to some extent"
"It is true, I never assisted the sun materially in his rising"
"To increase the warmth of our bodies by addition"
"The mass of men lead lives of quiet desperation"
"Conclusion"

The Massachusetts Review

"It is best to avoid the beginnings of evil"
"It is, after all, always the first person that is speaking"

Thanks to the Smith College Museum of Art for granting permission to reproduce Rockwell Kent's beautiful painting "Dublin Pond."

And enormous thanks to Ross White and Noah Stetzer for their response to this collaborative project and for giving these erasures such a wonderful home.

About the Authors

Matt Donovan is the author of four books and two chapbooks, including, most recently, *The Dug-Up Gun Museum* (BOA) and *Missing Department* (Visual Studies Workshop), a collection of poetry and art made in collaboration with artist Ligia Bouton. He is the recipient of a Whiting Award, a Rome Prize in Literature, a Creative Capital Grant, a Pushcart Prize, and an NEA Fellowship in Literature. Donovan serves as director of the Boutelle-Day Poetry Center at Smith College and lives in Amherst, Massachusetts.

Jenny George is the author of *The Dream of Reason* and *After Image*, both from Copper Canyon Press, as well as the chapbook * (Bull City Press). She has received support from the Bread Loaf Writers' Conference, the Iowa Writers' Workshop, Lannan Foundation, MacDowell, and Yaddo. Her poems have appeared in *Kenyon Review*, the *New York Times*, *Ploughshares*, *Poetry*, and elsewhere. She lives in Santa Fe, New Mexico, where she works in social justice philanthropy.

Also by Matt Donovan

The Dug-Up Gun Museum

Missing Department (with Ligia Bouton)

A Cloud of Unusual Size and Shape: Meditations on Ruin and Redemption

Rapture & the Big Bam

Vellum

Also by Jenny George

After Image

*

The Dream of Reason